The Ultimate Sausage Making Cookbook

Delicious Homemade Sausages for Every Occasion, from Breakfast to Dinner and Everything in Between. Discover the Art of Sausage Making with 100 Flavorful Recipes, Tips, and Techniques for Perfecting Your Craft

Christina Price

Copyright Material ©2023

All Rights Reserved

Without the proper written consent of the publisher and copyright owner, this book cannot be used or distributed in any way, shape, or form, except for brief quotations used in a review. This book should not be considered a substitute for medical, legal, or other professional advice.

TABLE OF CONTENTS

TABLE OF CONTENTS	**3**
INTRODUCTION	**8**
1. American Beef Sausage	10
2. American Pennsylvania Dutch Sausage	12
3. American Pork Sausage	14
4. American Beef Sausage	16
5. American Creole Sausage (Chaurice)	18
6. American Deer Cuckolds	20
7. American Ginger Pork Sausage	22
8. American Louisiana Sausage	24
9. American Norfolk Sausage	26
10. American Pork Sausage (Creole-Style)	28
11. American Pork Sausage	30
12. American Pork And Veal Sausage	32
13. American Rosemary Sausage	34
14. American Spicy Pork And Veal Sausage	36
15. American Venison Sausage	38
16. Armenian Lamb Sausage	40
17. Armenian Vienna Sausage	42
18. Bavarian Bockwurst	44
19. Chinese Cantonese Sausage	46

20. Cuban Sausage	48
21. Danish Liverwurst	50
22. Danish Pork Sausage	52
23. Danish Oxford Horns	54
24. English Oxford Sausage	56
25. French Boudin Blanc De Paris	58
26. French Boudin Blanc Du Mans	60
27. French Boudin Blanc	62
28. French Boudin Noir	64
29. French Cervelat	66
30. French Chicken Sausage	68
31. French Country Beef Sausage	70
32. French Brandy Sausage	72
33. French Style Chorizo	74
34. French Garlic Sausage	76
35. French Saucisses D'alsace-Lorraine	78
36. French Saucisses Cervelas	80
37. French Saucisses De Champagne	82
38. French Saucisses Au Champagne	84
39. French Saucisses Cuit Au Madère	86
40. French Saucisses Au Cumin	88
41. French Saucisses Espagnoles	90
42. French Saucisses De France	92

43. French Saucisses Au Foie De Porc	94
44. French Saucisses Du Perigord	96
45. French Saucisses De Toulouse	98
46. French Saucisses Viennoises	100
47. French White Chicken Pudding	102
48. German Black Pudding	104
49. German Black Pudding With Eggs	106
50. German Blood And Tongue Sausage	108
51. German Bockwurst	110
52. German Braunschweiger	112
53. German Bratwurst	114
54. German Frankfurters (Wieners)	116
55. German Frankfurter (Wienerwurst)	118
56. German Gehirnwurst	120
57. German Knackwurst	122
58. German Konigswurst	124
59. German knockwurst	126
60. German Liverwurst	128
61. German Mettwurst	130
62. German Metz	132
63. German Schwabischewurst	134
64. German Wurstchen	136
65. Greek Loukanika Sausage	138

66. Greek Orange Sausage	140
67. Greek Pork Sausage	142
68. Greek Blood Sausage	144
69. Hungarian Fish Sausage	146
70. Hungarian Hazi Kolbasz	148
71. Hungarian Hurka	150
72. Hungarian Kolbasz	152
73. Hungarian Majas Hurka (Hot Liver Sausage)	154
74. Irish Sausage	156
75. Irish Bologna	158
76. Italian Cooked Salami	161
77. Italian Cotechino	163
78. Italian Luganega	165
79. Italian Pepper Sausage	167
80. Italian Sausage	169
81. Italian Sausage (Hot)	171
82. Italian Sausage (Sweet)	173
83. Italian Sausage (Sweet Or Hot)	175
84. Italian chorizo	177
85. Mexican Sonora Chorizo	179
86. Mexican Chorizo	181
87. Mexican/Spanish Lamb Sausage	183
88. Norwegian Sausage	185

89. Polish Blood Sausage	187
90. Polish Kielbasa	189
91. Polish Kiszka	191
92. Polish Kiszka z Krwia	193
93. Polish Sausage	195
94. Smoked Polish Kielbasa	197
95. Portuguese Linguiça	199
96. Romanian Beef Sausage	201
97. Romanian Mititei	203
98. Romanian Pork And Beef Sausage	205
99. Russian Sausage	207
100. Scottish Haggis	209
CONCLUSION	**212**

INTRODUCTION

Welcome to The Ultimate Sausage Making Cookbook, where you'll find 100 mouth-watering sausage recipes that will take your culinary skills to the next level. Whether you're a novice or an experienced cook, you'll find plenty of inspiration and helpful tips in this comprehensive guide.

Each recipe is accompanied by a full-color photo, so you can see exactly what your sausage should look like. You'll also find detailed instructions on how to prepare and cook each sausage, as well as advice on choosing the right ingredients and equipment.

From classic Italian sausages to spicy chorizo and breakfast sausages, there's something for everyone in this cookbook. You'll also find recipes for vegetarian sausages, so even those who don't eat meat can enjoy the delicious flavors and textures of homemade sausages

With the rise of the handcrafted food movement, food lovers are going crazy for the all-natural, uniquely flavored, handmade sausages they're finding in butcher cases everywhere. Use this guide to take the craft of sausage making to a whole new level with fiery chorizo, maple-bacon breakfast links, smoky bratwurst, creamy boding blanc, and best-ever all-natural sandwich. This comprehensive, all-in-one manual welcomes a new generation of meat lovers and DIY enthusiasts to one of the most satisfying and tasty culinary crafts.

Happy Sausage-Making!

1. American Beef Sausage

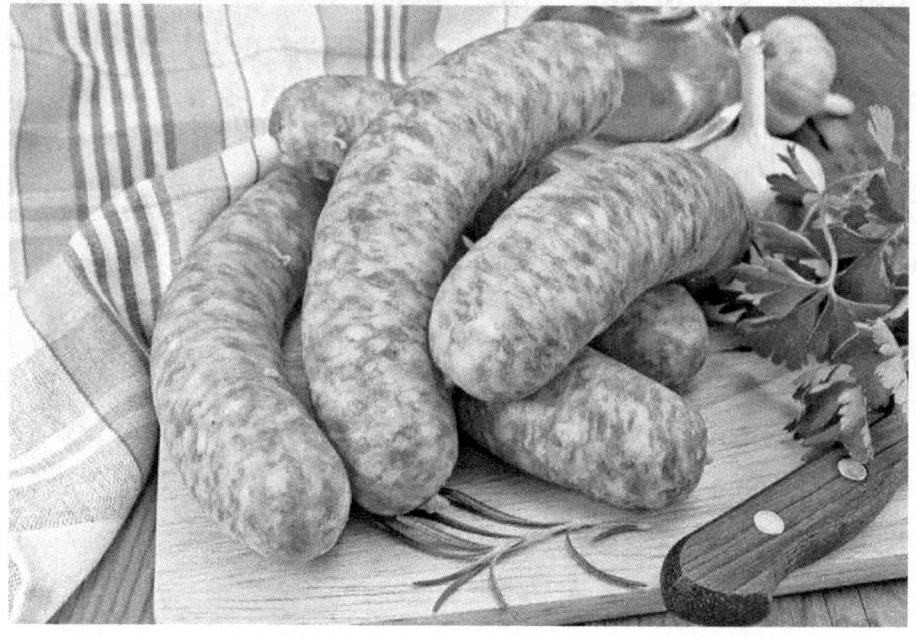

INGREDIENTS:
- 6 pounds lean ground beef
- 2 teaspoons sage
- 3 teaspoons salt
- $1\frac{1}{2}$ teaspoons freshly ground black pepper
- 1 teaspoon cayenne
- 3 cups bread crumbs
- 4 tablespoons parsley, chopped
- 2 beaten eggs
- 1 cup water

INSTRUCTIONS:
a) Mix all ingredients thoroughly and stuff into hog casings.
b) Put into boiling water, being sure to cover completely with water, and boil for about $\frac{1}{2}$ hour.
c) Take from pot and allow to cool, then refrigerate.
d) To serve, cut meat into thin slices and broil slowly until brown on all sides.

2. American Pennsylvania Dutch Sausage

INGREDIENTS:
- 5 pounds coarse ground pork butt
- ⅓ cup sage
- 2 tablespoons ground cloves
- 3 tablespoons coriander
- 2 tablespoons salt
- 1 tablespoon black pepper
- 1 cup cold water

INSTRUCTIONS:
a)   Combine all ingredients, mix well, and stuff into sheep casing.
b)   To cook, fry or bake.

3. American Pork Sausage

INGREDIENTS:
- 5 pounds medium ground pork
- 1 tablespoon salt
- 2 tablespoons sage
- 2 teaspoons freshly ground pepper
- 1 teaspoon ground cloves
- 2 teaspoons ground mace
- 2 teaspoons coriander
- 1 whole nutmeg, grated
- 1 cup water

INSTRUCTIONS:
a) Combine all ingredients, mix well, and stuff into sheep casing or make into patties.

4. American Beef Sausage

INGREDIENTS:
- 5 pounds medium ground beef chuck
- 2 teaspoons white pepper
- 2 teaspoons ground nutmeg
- 2 teaspoons sage
- 2 tablespoons sugar
- 4 cloves pressed garlic
- 2 tablespoons salt
- 1 cup water

INSTRUCTIONS:
a) Combine all ingredients, mix well, and stuff into sheep casing.
b) To cook, bake, broil, or fry.

5. American Creole Sausage (Chaurice)

INGREDIENTS:
- 5 pounds coarse ground pork butt
- 1 cup grated onions
- 8 cloves pressed garlic
- 1 tablespoon dried hot crushed peppers
- 3 teaspoons cayenne
- 2 teaspoons black pepper
- 1 teaspoon allspice
- 2 teaspoons sugar
- 1 tablespoon salt
- 1 cup chopped parsley
- 1 cup cold water

INSTRUCTIONS:
a) Combine all ingredients, mix well, and stuff into hog casing.
b) To cook, broil, bake, or fry.

6. American Deer Cuckolds

INGREDIENTS:
- Deer stomach
- 3 ounces suet
- 1 onion
- 8 ounces venison
- 3 ounces oatmeal
- salt & pepper

INSTRUCTIONS:
a) Mix above ingredients. Wash deer stomach and turn inside out.
b) Fill the stomach with mixture, then tie at both ends. Boil for 45 minutes.
c) When you are ready to eat this unusual sausage, fry it in hot fat until brown, about 15 minutes. Serve piping hot.

7. American Ginger Pork Sausage

INGREDIENTS:
- 5 pounds medium ground pork butt
- 5 teaspoons salt
- 3 teaspoons black pepper
- 2 teaspoons ground ginger

INSTRUCTIONS:
a) Combine all ingredients, mix well, and stuff into hog casing.
b) To cook, pan-fry.

8. American Louisiana Sausage

INGREDIENTS:
- 5 pounds medium ground pork butt
- 5 teaspoons salt
- 2 teaspoons black pepper
- $\frac{1}{2}$ teaspoons allspice
- 2 teaspoons thyme
- $1\frac{1}{2}$ teaspoons cayenne
- $1\frac{1}{2}$ teaspoons chili pepper
- 1 large minced onion
- 4 cloves pressed garlic
- 1 cup cold water

INSTRUCTIONS:
a) Combine all ingredients, mix well, and stuff into hog casing or make patties.

9. American Norfolk Sausage

INGREDIENTS:
- 5 pounds medium ground beef chuck
- 1½ tablespoons salt
- 2 cups grated parmesan cheese
- 1½ tablespoons black pepper
- 1 tablespoon basil
- 1 tablespoon oregano
- 3 teaspoons mustard seed
- 8 cloves pressed garlic
- 1 small grated onion
- 1½ cups red wine

INSTRUCTIONS:
a) Combine all ingredients, mix well, and stuff into hog casing.
b) To cook, bake or broil (also, barbecue slowly).

10. <u>American Pork Sausage (Creole-Style)</u>

INGREDIENTS:
- 5 pounds medium ground pork
- 2 chopped large onions
- 1 clove garlic, minced
- 3 teaspoons salt
- 2 teaspoons freshly ground pepper
- 1 teaspoon crushed, dried chili pepper
- 2 teaspoons paprika
- $\frac{1}{2}$ teaspoons cayenne
- 2 tablespoons parsley, chopped
- $\frac{1}{4}$ teaspoons ground allspice
- $\frac{1}{4}$ teaspoons thyme
- $1\frac{1}{2}$ cups water

INSTRUCTIONS:
a) Combine all ingredients, mix well, and stuff into sheep casing.
b) Refrigerate.
c) To cook, pan-fry over medium heat until brown on all sides and cook until well done.

11. American Pork Sausage

INGREDIENTS:
- 5 pounds medium ground pork
- 1 tablespoon freshly ground black pepper
- ½ cup ground sage
- 2 tablespoons salt
- 1 cup water

INSTRUCTIONS:
a) Combine all ingredients, mix well, and stuff into hog casing.
b) Smoke sausages until skin seems dry and hard. Hang sausage in dry place until ready to use.
c) To cook, slice sausages down middle, lengthwise, and broil slowly, browning both sides until well done.

12. American Pork And Veal Sausage

INGREDIENTS:
- 4 pounds medium ground pork butt
- 1 pounds medium ground veal
- 2 cups bread crumbs
- 3 tablespoons salt
- $1\frac{1}{2}$ tablespoons ground allspice
- 1 teaspoon thyme
- 1 teaspoon sage
- $1\frac{1}{2}$ teaspoons black pepper
- 1 cup water

INSTRUCTIONS:
a) Combine all ingredients, mix well, and stuff into hog or sheep casing.
b) To cook, fry in hot fat.

13. American Rosemary Sausage

INGREDIENTS:
- 1½ pounds fine ground veal
- 2 pounds fine ground pork butt
- 1½ pounds fine ground beef chuck
- 2 teaspoons black pepper
- 1½ tablespoons salt
- 1 tablespoon rosemary
- 1 teaspoon nutmeg
- 1 teaspoon thyme
- 1 teaspoon marjoram
- 1 cup water

INSTRUCTIONS:
a) Combine all ingredients, mix well, and stuff into hog casing.
b) Bake, fry, or broil.

14. American Spicy Pork And Veal Sausage

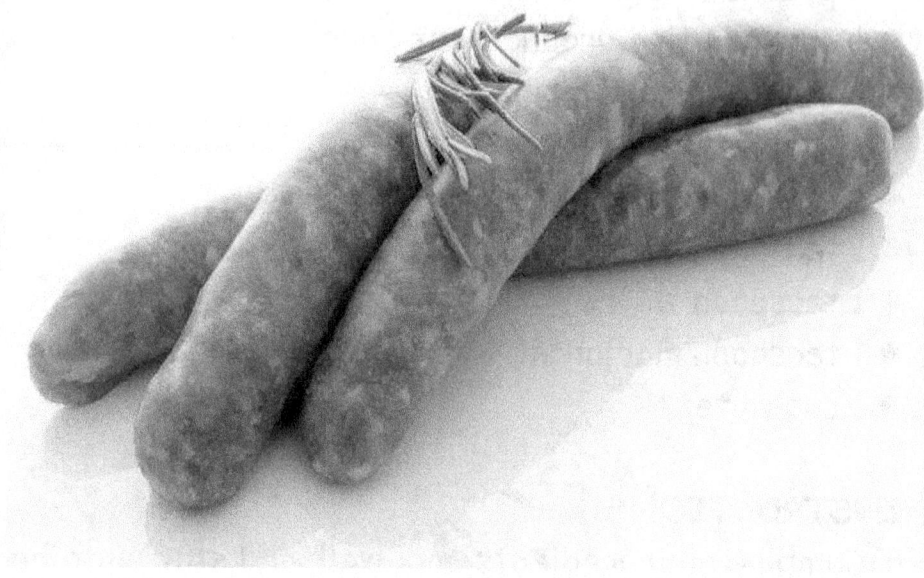

INGREDIENTS:
- 4 pounds fine ground pork butt
- 1 pounds fine ground veal
- 1 cup potato flour
- 4 cups water
- 2 tablespoons salt
- $1\frac{1}{2}$ teaspoons white pepper
- 2 tablespoons sugar
- $\frac{1}{2}$ teaspoons ground cloves
- $\frac{1}{2}$ teaspoons ground ginger

INSTRUCTIONS:
a) Combine all ingredients, mix well, and stuff into hog casing. Sprinkle with equal parts salt and sugar.
b) Refrigerate at least 24 hours. Poach about 20 minutes, then broil or fry.

15. American Venison Sausage

INGREDIENTS:
- 4 pounds coarse ground venison
- 1 pounds fine ground bacon
- 1 tablespoon salt
- 1 tablespoon sage
- 1 teaspoon allspice
- 2 tablespoons sugar
- 1 teaspoon coriander
- $1\frac{1}{2}$ teaspoons mustard seed
- 6 cloves pressed garlic
- 2 tablespoons black pepper
- 1 cup cold water

INSTRUCTIONS:
a) Combine all ingredients, mix thoroughly, and stuff into hog casing.
b) To cook, boil, bake, or fry.

16. Armenian Lamb Sausage

INGREDIENTS:
- 5 pounds medium ground lamb
- 1 cup finely chopped onion
- 8 cloves pressed garlic
- 2 teaspoons black pepper
- 1 tablespoon salt
- ⅔ cup fresh mint leaves
- 1 cup water

INSTRUCTIONS:
a) Combine all ingredients, mix well, and stuff into sheep casing.
b) To cook, broil or barbecue.

17. Armenian Vienna Sausage

INGREDIENTS:
- 3½ pounds fine ground pork butt
- 2½ pounds fine ground beef stew meat
- ¼ cup fine chopped onions
- 2 teaspoons sugar
- 1 teaspoon cayenne
- 2 teaspoons paprika
- 1 teaspoon ground mace
- 1 tablespoon ground coriander
- 1½ tablespoons salt
- ¼ cup arrow root
- 1½ cups milk

INSTRUCTIONS:
a) Combine all ingredients, mix well, and put through the fine blade of the grinder again.
b) Stuff into sheep casing. Do not separate links.
c) Place in hot water and simmer approximately 45 minutes.
d) Remove, cool, and store.

18. Bavarian Bockwurst

INGREDIENTS:
- 3 pounds fine ground veal
- 2 pounds fine ground pork butt
- 1½ cups cream
- ⅓ cup chopped chives
- 1 cup grated onion
- 1½ tablespoons white pepper
- 1 tablespoon salt
- ¾ teaspoons nutmeg
- ½ teaspoons mace
- 1 cup water

INSTRUCTIONS:
a) Combine all ingredients, mix well, and stuff into hog casing.
b) Simmer 20 minutes, then fry.

19. Chinese Cantonese Sausage

INGREDIENTS:
- 5 pounds coarse ground pork butt
- 1 tablespoon salt
- $\frac{1}{2}$ cup honey
- $\frac{1}{4}$ cup orange juice
- 2 tablespoons white vinegar
- 1 cup soy sauce
- 1 cup rice wine

INSTRUCTIONS:
a) Combine all ingredients, mix well, and stuff into hog casing.
b) To cook, fry in peanut oil.

20. Cuban Sausage

INGREDIENTS:
- 5 pounds coarse ground pork butt
- 1½ tablespoons salt
- 1 tablespoon black pepper
- 8 cloves pressed garlic
- 2 teaspoons cumin
- 3 teaspoons oregano
- ¾ cup annatto or paprika
- 2 cups water

INSTRUCTIONS:
a) Combine all ingredients, mix well, and stuff into hog casing.
b) To cook, barbecue, broil, or fry.

21. Danish Liverwurst

INGREDIENTS:
- 4 pounds fine ground cooked pork liver (boiled)
- 1 pounds fine ground bacon
- 2 cups minced onions
- $1\frac{1}{2}$ cups milk
- $1\frac{1}{2}$ cups evaporated milk
- $\frac{1}{2}$ cup potato flour
- 6 beaten eggs
- 3 teaspoons black pepper
- 2 tablespoons salt
- 1 teaspoon ground cloves
- 1 teaspoon allspice

INSTRUCTIONS:
a) Make a sauce of the milk and potato flour, and cook until thick.
b) Combine all ingredients.
c) Simmer in salted water for approximately 20 minutes.
d) Refrigerate for 24 hours before using.
e) Split sausage and use like a spread.

22. Danish Pork Sausage

INGREDIENTS:
- 5 pounds fine ground pork butt
- 5 teaspoons salt
- ¼ teaspoons allspice
- 2 teaspoons white pepper
- ¼ teaspoons cloves
- 1 teaspoon cardamom
- 1 large minced onion
- 1 cup cold beef bouillon

INSTRUCTIONS:
a) Combine all ingredients, mix well, and stuff into hog casing.

23. Danish Oxford Horns

INGREDIENTS:
- 5 pounds coarse ground pork butt
- 1½ tablespoons sage
- 1½ teaspoons thyme
- 1½ teaspoons marjoram
- whole grated lemon peel
- 1½ teaspoons nutmeg
- 4 teaspoons salt
- 2 teaspoons black pepper
- 3 eggs
- 1 cup water

INSTRUCTIONS:
a) Combine all ingredients, mix well, and stuff into hog casing.
b) To cook, panfry or broil.

24. English Oxford Sausage

INGREDIENTS:
- 2 pounds fine ground pork butt
- 2 pounds fine ground veal
- 1 pounds fine ground beef chuck
- ½ loaf fresh sourdough bread crumbs
- 1½ whole grated lemon peel
- 1 teaspoon thyme
- 1 teaspoon sage
- 1 teaspoon savory
- 1 teaspoon rosemary
- 1 whole nutmeg, grated
- 4 teaspoons salt
- 2 teaspoons salt
- 2 teaspoons black pepper
- 1 cup water
- 4 eggs

INSTRUCTIONS:
a) Combine all ingredients, mix well, and stuff into hog casing.
b) To cook, panfry or broil.

25. French Boudin Blanc De Paris

INGREDIENTS:
- 2½ pounds fine ground pork butt
- 2½ pounds fine ground chicken breast
- 2 tablespoons salt
- 2½ teaspoons white pepper
- 1 teaspoon quatre-epices
- 6 cups finely chopped onions
- 1½ cups bread crumbs soaked in 1 cup hot cream
- 8 eggs

INSTRUCTIONS:
a) Combine all ingredients, mix well, and stuff into hog casing.
b) To cook, panfry or broil.

26. French Boudin Blanc Du Mans

INGREDIENTS:
- 5 pounds fine ground pork butt
- 2 tablespoons salt
- 3 teaspoons quatre-epices
- 1½ cups finely chopped onions
- ¾ cup chopped parsley
- 2 cups cream
- 4 eggs

INSTRUCTIONS:
a) Combine all ingredients, mix well, and stuff into hog casing.
b) To cook, panfry or broil.

27. French Boudin Blanc

INGREDIENTS:
- 2½ pounds fine ground pork butt
- 2½ pounds fine ground chicken breast
- 2 tablespoons salt
- 3 teaspoons white pepper
- 3 teaspoons quatre-epices
- 20 eggs
- 6 tablespoons rice flour and 6 cups milk, mixed together—avoid lumps

INSTRUCTIONS:
a) Combine all ingredients, mix well, and stuff into hog casing.
b) To cook, panfry or broil.

28. <u>French Boudin Noir</u>

INGREDIENTS:
- 2 pounds coarse ground cooked pork butt
- 3 pints hog or beef blood
- 2 cups fried onions
- 1 tablespoon salt
- 2 teaspoons black pepper
- 2 teaspoons cayenne
- 4 cloves pressed garlic
- $\frac{1}{2}$ teaspoons ground allspice
- $\frac{1}{2}$ teaspoons ground mace
- $\frac{1}{2}$ teaspoons ground cloves
- $\frac{1}{2}$ teaspoons ground nutmeg

INSTRUCTIONS:
a) Combine all ingredients, mix well, and stuff into hog casing.

b) To cook, place sausage in tepid water and simmer for 15 minutes.

c) Also, you can bake it.

29. French Cervelat

INGREDIENTS:
- 4 pounds medium ground pork butt
- 1 pounds fine ground bacon
- 1 cup chopped parsley
- $\frac{1}{4}$ cup chopped scallions and greens
- $1\frac{1}{2}$ tablespoons salt
- 1 teaspoon thyme
- 1 teaspoon basil
- 6 cloves pressed garlic
- 1 cup dry white wine

INSTRUCTIONS:
a) Combine all ingredients and stuff into casing. Hang for 3-4 days in a cool place.

b) Cook this sausage in beef bouillon for at least three hours with salt, black pepper, thyme, basil, bay leaf, parsley, and chopped scallions.

30. French Chicken Sausage

INGREDIENTS:
- 4 pounds medium ground cooked white chicken
- 1 pounds medium ground cooked bacon
- 1 pounds medium ground cooked chicken livers
- 10 medium eggs
- 1 tablespoon salt
- 1 teaspoon nutmeg
- 1 teaspoon ground cloves
- 2 teaspoons white pepper
- 1 cup chicken bouillon
- 1 cup bread crumbs

INSTRUCTIONS:
a) Combine all ingredients, mix well, and stuff into sheep casing.
b) To cook, broil, bake, or fry in butter.

31. French Country Beef Sausage

INGREDIENTS:
- 4 pounds lean beef
- 2 pounds lean bacon
- $2\frac{1}{2}$ tablespoons salt
- 3 teaspoons freshly ground pepper
- 4 cloves pressed garlic
- 2 tablespoons pimento, chopped
- 1 cup water

INSTRUCTIONS:
a) Grind beef with fine plate of grinder along with the bacon.
b) Mix well with other ingredients and stuff into sheep casing.
c) You may tie every 4-6 inches.
d) Dry in warm oven or smoke very lightly.
e) To serve, poach in boiling water or beef stock for about 10-12 minutes.

32. French Brandy Sausage

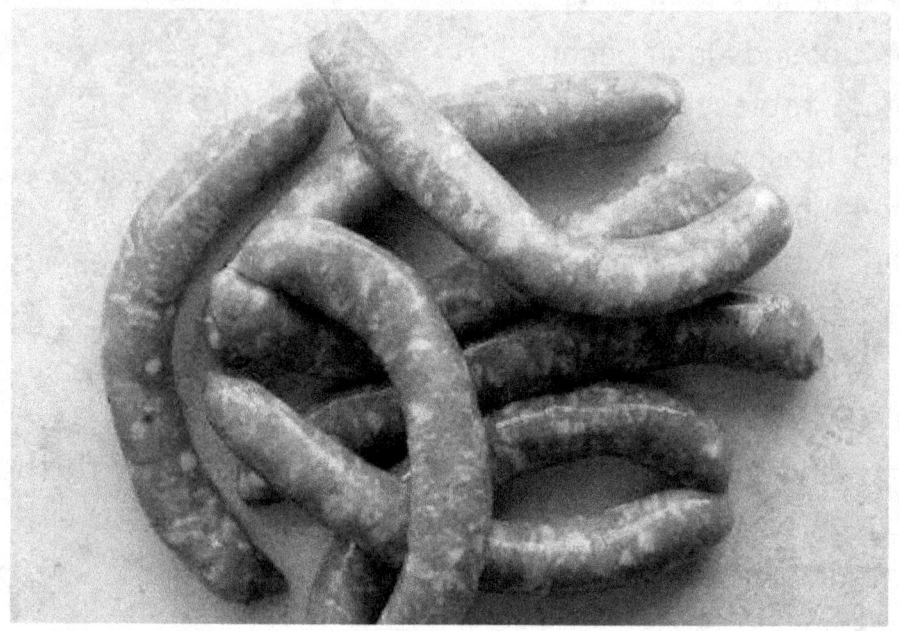

INGREDIENTS:
- 2 pounds fine ground veal
- 2 pounds fine ground pork
- 1 pounds fine ground beef
- 4 cloves garlic, pressed
- 1 large minced onion
- 1 cup finely chopped parsley
- 5 teaspoons salt
- 5 teaspoons pepper
- 1 cup California brandy

INSTRUCTIONS:
a) Combine all ingredients, mix well and stuff into hog casing.
b) Sprinkle with equal parts salt and brown sugar. Refrigerate at least overnight.
c) Scald to cook and fry.

33. French Style Chorizo

INGREDIENTS:
- 5 pounds coarse ground pork butt
- 2 tablespoons salt
- 1 teaspoon sugar
- 2 chopped large sweet peppers
- 1 teaspoon quatre-epices
- 2 teaspoons cayenne pepper
- 4 large cloves pressed garlic
- 1 cup red wine

INSTRUCTIONS:
a) Combine all ingredients, mix well, and stuff into hog casing.
b) Tie every 6 inches. Cool smoke lightly for 8-10 hours.
c) To cook, fry or grill.

34. French Garlic Sausage

INGREDIENTS:
- 5 pounds medium ground pork butt
- $1\frac{1}{2}$ tablespoons salt
- $1\frac{1}{2}$ teaspoons black pepper
- $\frac{1}{2}$ teaspoons cayenne
- $\frac{1}{2}$ teaspoons nutmeg
- $\frac{1}{2}$ teaspoons cloves
- $\frac{1}{2}$ teaspoons cinnamon
- 8 cloves pressed garlic
- $\frac{1}{4}$ cup brandy
- 1 cup water

INSTRUCTIONS:
a) Combine all ingredients, mix well, and stuff into hog casing.
b) To cook, broil or fry.

35. French Saucisses D'alsace-Lorraine

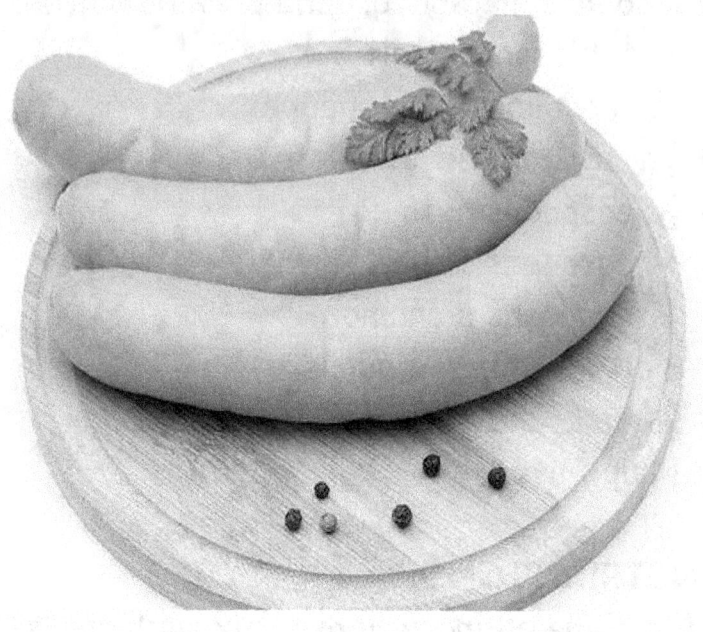

INGREDIENTS:
- 5 pounds medium ground pork butt
- 2 tablespoons salt
- $\frac{1}{4}$ teaspoons ground ginger
- 1 teaspoon sugar
- 1 teaspoon black pepper
- 1 teaspoon quatre-epices
- 1 cup white wine
- 3 cups finely chopped mushrooms

INSTRUCTIONS:
a) Combine all ingredients, mix well, and stuff into sheep casing.
b) Tie every 6 inches.
c) To cook, fry in butter.

36. French Saucisses Cervelas

INGREDIENTS:
- 3 pounds medium ground pork butt
- 1 pounds medium ground beef chuck
- 1 pounds fine ground bacon
- 2 tablespoons salt
- 1 tablespoon black pepper
- 8 cloves pressed garlic
- 1 large onion, minced
- 1 cup water

INSTRUCTIONS:
a) Combine all ingredients, mix well, and stuff into hog casing.
b) Tie every 6 or 10 inches. It can be smoked if you like.
c) To cook, simmer in hot water or red wine.

37. French Saucisses De Champagne

INGREDIENTS:
- 5 pounds coarse ground pork butt
- 2 tablespoons salt
- 2 teaspoons sugar
- 2 teaspoons black pepper
- 2 teaspoons quatre-epices
- 1 teaspoon thyme
- 1 cup chopped parsley
- $\frac{1}{2}$ cup pimentos
- 4 cloves pressed garlic
- 1 cup red wine

INSTRUCTIONS:
a) Combine all ingredients, mix well, and stuff into large sheep casing. Tie every 6 inches.

b) Poach the sausage in simmering water for 15-20 minutes, then fry in butter or grill.

38. French Saucisses Au Champagne

INGREDIENTS:
- 5 pounds fine ground pork butt
- 2 tablespoons salt
- 2½ teaspoons quatre-epices
- 6 fresh eggs
- 3 cups finely chopped mushrooms
- 1 bottle champagne

INSTRUCTIONS:
a) Combine all ingredients, mix well, and stuff into large sheep casing.
b) Tie every 6 inches.
c) Poach the sausage in simmering water for 15-20 minutes, then fry in butter or grill.

39. French Saucisses Cuit Au Madère

INGREDIENTS:
- 5 pounds fine ground pork butt
- 2 tablespoons salt
- $1\frac{1}{2}$ teaspoons quatre-epices
- 2 cups chopped mushrooms
- 4 ounces pistachio nuts, chopped
- 1 cup Madeira wine

INSTRUCTIONS:
a) Combine all ingredients, mix well, and stuff into hog casing.
b) Tie every 6 inches.
c) Simmer for 1 hour, cool, and store in the refrigerator.
d) To cook, bake.

40. French Saucisses Au Cumin

INGREDIENTS:
- 2½ pounds medium ground pork butt
- 2½ pounds fine ground beef chuck
- 4 tablespoons salt
- 10 cloves pressed garlic
- 1 tablespoon black pepper
- 2 tablespoons chopped peppers
- 4 tablespoons ground cumin
- 1 cup water

INSTRUCTIONS:
a) Combine all ingredients, mix well, and stuff into hog casing.
b) Tie every 5 inches. Cool smoke for 48 hours.
c) Dry another 5 days.
d) To cook, fry, grill, or boil.

41. French Saucisses Espagnoles

INGREDIENTS:
- 5 pounds medium ground pork butt
- 2 tablespoons salt
- 3 tablespoons sweet red pepper, crushed
- 3 teaspoons quatre-epices
- 2 teaspoons cayenne pepper
- 1 cup raisins, chopped
- 1 cup red wine

INSTRUCTIONS:
a) Combine all ingredients, mix well, and stuff into hog casing.
b) Tie every 5 inches.
c) Cool smoke for 8-12 hours.
d) To cook, fry or grill.

42. French Saucisses De France

INGREDIENTS:
- 5 pounds medium ground pork butt
- 2 tablespoons salt
- 2 teaspoons quatre-epices
- 2 teaspoons black pepper
- 1 cup chopped parsley
- 1 teaspoon sage
- 1 teaspoon thyme
- 1 cup white wine

INSTRUCTIONS:
a) Combine all ingredients, mix well, and stuff into hog casing.
b) Tie off every 4-6 inches.
c) Poach for an hour, then cool. To cook, fry or grill.

43. French Saucisses Au Foie De Porc

INGREDIENTS:
- 3 pounds medium ground pork butt
- 2 pounds mashed pork liver
- 1 pounds sauteed chopped onions
- 2 tablespoons salt
- 2 teaspoons black pepper
- 2 teaspoons quatre-epices
- 1 cup Kirschwasser or brandy

INSTRUCTIONS:
a) Combine all ingredients, mix well, and stuff into hog casing.
b) Tie off every 4-6 inches.
c) Poach for an hour, then cool. To cook, fry or grill.

44. French Saucisses Du Perigord

INGREDIENTS:
- 5 pounds medium ground pork butt
- 2 tablespoons salt
- 2 cups chopped mushrooms
- or truffles
- 2 teaspoons sugar
- 2 teaspoons black pepper
- 2 teaspoons quatre-epices
- 1 cup white wine

INSTRUCTIONS:
a) Combine all ingredients, mix well, and stuff into sheep casing.
b) Tie off every 5 inches.
c) To cook, fry in butter.

45. French Saucisses De Toulouse

INGREDIENTS:
- 5 pounds coarse ground pork butt
- 2 tablespoons salt
- 3 tablespoons sugar
- 1 teaspoon quatre-epices
- 1 cup water

INSTRUCTIONS:
a) Combine all ingredients, mix well, and stuff into hog casing.
b) Tie off every 6-8 inches. To cook, fry or grill.

46. French Saucisses Viennoises

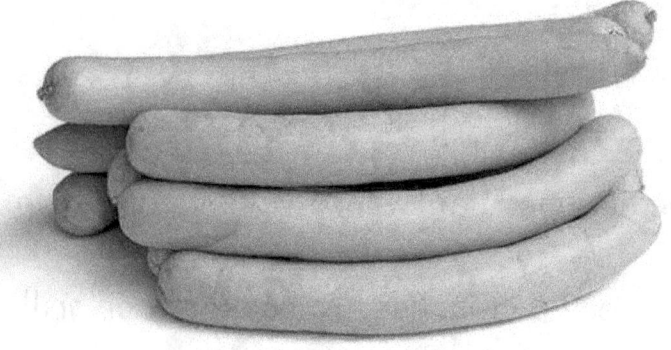

INGREDIENTS:
- 2 pounds fine ground pork butt
- 2 pounds fine ground beef chuck
- 1 pounds fine ground veal
- 2 tablespoons salt
- 1 teaspoon quatre-epices
- 2 teaspoons cayenne pepper
- 2 teaspoons coriander
- 2 cups water

INSTRUCTIONS:
a) Combine all ingredients, mix well, and stuff into lamb or small hog casing.
b) Cold smoke for 8-10 hours.
c) To cook, fry, grill, or boil.

47. French White Chicken Pudding

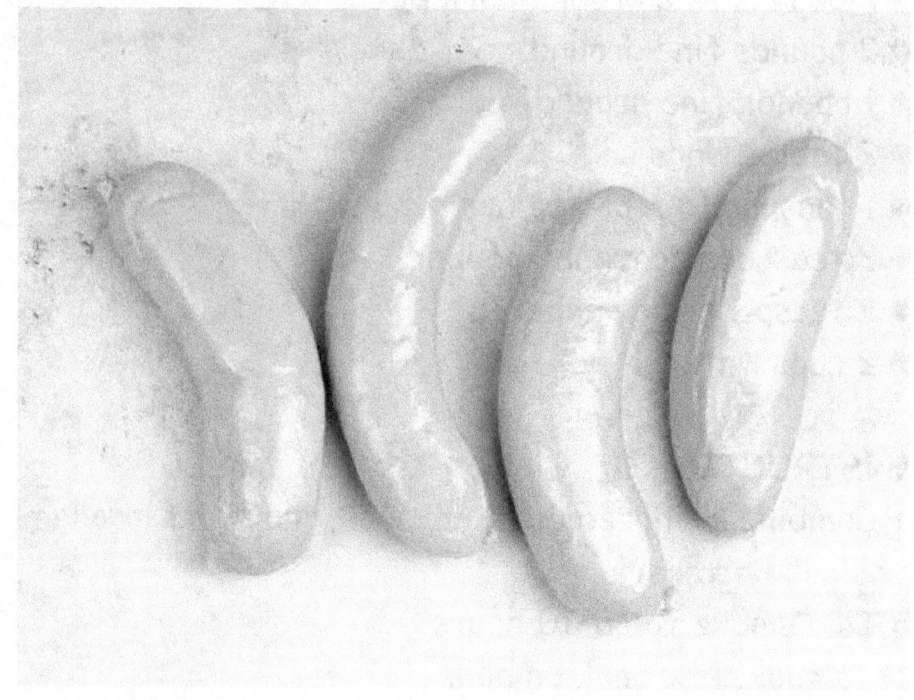

INGREDIENTS:
- 3 pounds fine ground chicken breast
- 2 pounds fine ground pork butt
- 1 cup chopped onions, sauteed in butter
- 3 bay leaves
- 1 teaspoon thyme
- 5 tablespoons salt
- 1 teaspoon white pepper
- 1 teaspoon mace
- 1 teaspoon nutmeg
- 8 eggs
- 4 cups scalded milk, chilled

INSTRUCTIONS:
a) Combine all ingredients, mix well, and stuff into hog casing.
b) To cook, simmer for 20 minutes, then broil with butter under low heat.

48. German Black Pudding

INGREDIENTS:
- 4 pounds pork fat, cubed
- 4 cups onion, chopped and lightly
- sauteed in lard
- 4 teaspoons salt
- ½ teaspoons freshly ground black pepper
- ½ teaspoons ground all spice
- 2 cups cream
- 8 cups pig's blood

INSTRUCTIONS:
a) Mix above ingredients well. Stuff into casing rather loosely.

b) Place puddings in wire basket or similar contraption and plunge into boiling water. Reduce heat and simmer for 20 minutes.

c) As puddings rise to surface of water, prick skins with needle to release air. Drain and allow to cool in container.

d) To serve, make a few slight incisions in both sides of puddings and broil slowly under low heat, making sure to brown on all sides.

49. German Black Pudding With Eggs

INGREDIENTS:
- 2 pounds pork fat, cubed and slightly melted
- 1 cup cream
- 6 eggs, beaten
- 1 cup onion, lightly sauteed in fat
- 1 tablespoon salt
- $\frac{1}{2}$ teaspoons freshly ground black pepper
- $\frac{1}{2}$ teaspoons allspice, ground
- $\frac{1}{2}$ teaspoons thyme
- bay leaves, crushed
- 4 cups pig's blood

INSTRUCTIONS:
a) Mix above ingredients well. Stuff into hog casing, making sure to stuff loosely as this mixture will swell when poaching.

b) Place puddings in wire basket and put into boiling water.

c) Reduce heat to just below boiling and cook for about 20 minutes.

d) When the puddings rise to the surface, prick with needle to release air. To serve, split puddings and broil slowly under low heat until brown on all sides.

e) Add one teaspoons vinegar to one qt. of fresh blood to prevent it from coagulating.

50. German Blood And Tongue Sausage

INGREDIENTS:
- 9 pounds pork back fat
- 3 pounds cooked rinds
- 6 pounds cooked pork tongues
- 2 pounds blood
- 7 ounces salt
- $\frac{3}{4}$ ounces pepper
- $\frac{1}{2}$ ounces mace
- $\frac{1}{4}$ ounces marjoram
- $\frac{1}{4}$ ounces onion powder (optional)

INSTRUCTIONS:
a) Cube back fat and scald in boiling water.
b) Put cooked rinds through fine plate of grinder 2 times.
c) Cube the cooked, skinned tongues.
d) Place blood into container of hot water to heat a little.
e) Strain off water from pork fat and mix all ingredients together. They should be as hot as possible during the mixing procedure.
f) Stuff into ox (preferably) casing, plunge into boiling water and reduce heat to 180° F. Cook 3-4 hours depending on size of sausages.
g) Add one teaspoons vinegar per quart of fresh blood to keep it from coagulating.

51. German Bockwurst

INGREDIENTS:
- 4½ pounds fine ground veal
- ½ pounds fine ground pork fat
- ¾ cup finely chopped onions
- 3 cups milk
- 3 eggs
- 2½ teaspoons ground cloves
- 1½ teaspoons white pepper
- 3 teaspoons finely chopped parsley
- 3 teaspoons salt

INSTRUCTIONS:
a) Combine all ingredients, mix well, and put through the fine blade of the grinder again.
b) Stuff into hog casing.

52. German Braunschweiger

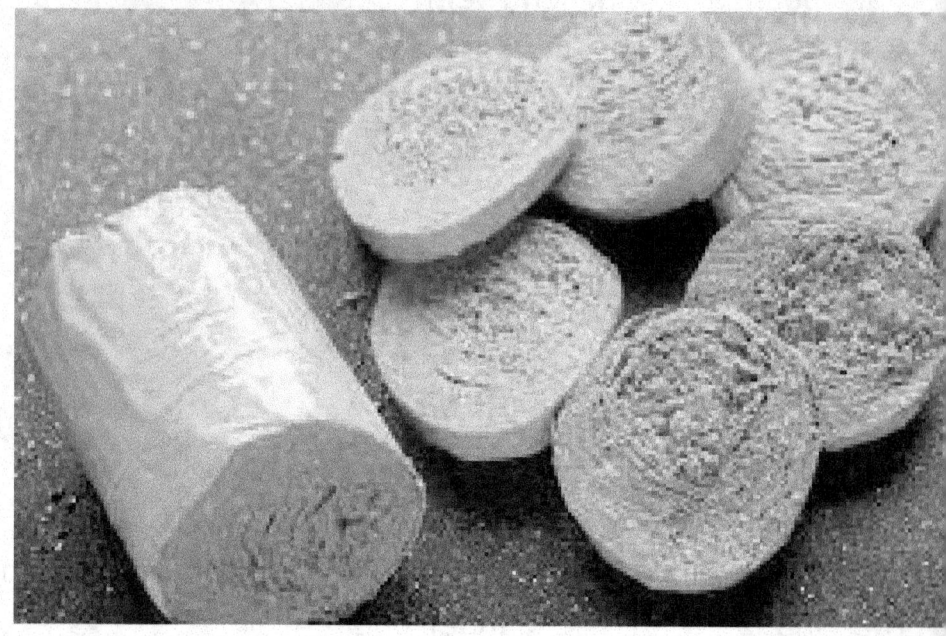

INGREDIENTS:
- 2½ pounds fine ground cooked pork liver (boiled)
- 2½ pounds fine ground cooked pork butt (boiled)
- 2 tablespoons salt
- 1 cup grated onions
- 1 tablespoon sugar
- 2 teaspoons white pepper
- 2 teaspoons ground cloves
- ½ teaspoons ground ginger
- 2 teaspoons ground nutmeg
- ½ teaspoons ground marjoram
- ¼ teaspoons sage
- ¼ teaspoons allspice
- 1 cup water used for boiling meat

INSTRUCTIONS:
a) Combine all ingredients, mix until smooth and pasty, and stuff into beef, hog, or cloth casing.
b) Simmer in salted water for approximately 20 minutes.
c) Refrigerate for 24 hours before using.
d) This sausage is much like liverwurst. Use it as a spread.

53. German Bratwurst

INGREDIENTS:
- 4 pounds fine ground pork butt
- 2 pounds fine ground veal
- $\frac{1}{2}$ teaspoons ground allspice
- 1 teaspoon caraway seeds
- 1 teaspoon dried marjoram
- $1\frac{1}{2}$ teaspoons white pepper
- 3 teaspoons salt
- 1 cup cold water

INSTRUCTIONS:
a) Combine all ingredients, mix well, and put through the fine blade of the grinder again.
b) Stuff into hog casing.

54. German Frankfurters (Wieners)

INGREDIENTS:
- 3 pounds fine ground beef chuck
- 2 pounds fine ground pork butt
- 2 teaspoons white pepper
- 1 teaspoon ground coriander
- 1 teaspoon ground ginger
- 1 teaspoon ground mace
- 4 cloves pressed garlic
- 1½ tablespoons salt
- 1½ cups water

INSTRUCTIONS:
a) Combine all ingredients, mix well, and stuff into sheep casing.

b) Smoke for 2 or 3 hours at 115°F or until a rich orange color is reached.

c) Then cook in water heated to 160°-170°F until frankfurters float.

55. German Frankfurter (Wienerwurst)

INGREDIENTS:
- 3½ pounds fine ground pork butt
- 1½ pounds fine ground beef stew meat
- ¾ cup finely chopped onions
- 3 cloves pressed garlic
- 2 teaspoons ground coriander
- ½ teaspoons marjoram
- ½ teaspoons ground mace
- ¾ teaspoons ground mustard
- 2 teaspoons paprika
- 2 teaspoons white pepper
- 2 egg whites
- 1 tablespoon sugar
- 1 tablespoon salt
- ½ cup milk
- 1 cup cold water

INSTRUCTIONS:
a) Puree all ingredients except the meat.
b) Mix well and put through the fine blade of the grinder again.
c) Add meat to mixture and stuff into small hog or sheep casing.
d) Parboil (w/o separating them) in simmering water for approximately 20 minutes.
e) Place in ice water, remove, and store.

56. German Gehirnwurst

INGREDIENTS:
- 2½ pounds pork brains (cooked in salted, acidulated water)
- 2½ pounds coarse ground pork
- 2 tablespoons salt
- 1 tablespoon pepper
- 2 teaspoons mace
- 1 cup water

INSTRUCTIONS:
a) Cook pork brains until done.
b) Combine all ingredients, mix well, and stuff into hog casing.
c) To cook, poach in boiling water, or fry or bake.

57. German Knackwurst

INGREDIENTS:
- 4 pounds medium ground pork
- 2 pounds beef
- 3 tablespoons salt
- 1½ tablespoons cumin
- 1 tablespoon garlic powder
- 1 cup water

INSTRUCTIONS:
a) Combine all ingredients and stuff into hog casing.
b) Dry 2 days in refrigerator, then cool smoke until the sausages turn an amber color.
c) Poach 10 minutes, then sauté in butter until nicely browned.

58. German Konigswurst

INGREDIENTS:
- 2½ pounds coarse ground chicken meat
- 2½ pounds partridge meat
- ¾ cup mushrooms, chopped
- 2 eggs
- 2 tablespoons salt
- 2 teaspoons pepper
- 2 teaspoons mace
- 1 cup Rhine wine

INSTRUCTIONS:
a) Combine all ingredients, mix well, and put into sheep casing.

b) To cook, panfry, or broil or bake until a nice golden brown on all sides.

59. German knockwurst

INGREDIENTS:
- 3 pounds fine ground beef chuck
- 2 pounds fine ground pork butt
- 2 tablespoons salt
- 2 teaspoons sugar
- $2\frac{1}{2}$ tablespoons white pepper
- 2 teaspoons mace
- $\frac{1}{4}$ teaspoons ground allspice
- $\frac{1}{2}$ teaspoons coriander
- 1 tablespoon paprika
- 4 cloves pressed garlic
- 1 cup water

INSTRUCTIONS:
a)   Combine all ingredients, mix well, and stuff into hog casing.
b)   To cook, bake or fry.

60. German Liverwurst

INGREDIENTS:
- 2½ pounds fine ground cooked pork liver (boiled)
- 2½ pounds fine ground cooked pork butt (boiled)
- 2 tablespoons salt
- 1 cup grated onions
- 1 tablespoon sugar
- 2¼ teaspoons white pepper
- ½ teaspoons ground sage
- ½ teaspoons marjoram
- ½ teaspoons ground nutmeg
- ¼ teaspoons ground ginger
- 1 cup water used to boil meat

INSTRUCTIONS:
a) Combine all ingredients, mix until smooth and pasty, and stuff into beef, hog, or cloth casing.

b) Simmer in salted water for approximately 20 minutes.

c) Refrigerate for 24 hours before using. Use as a spread.

61. German Mettwurst

INGREDIENTS:
- 3 pounds fine ground cooked pork butt (boiled)
- 2 pounds fine ground cooked pork liver (boiled)
- 1 tablespoon salt
- 3 teaspoons white pepper
- 3 teaspoons coriander
- 1 cup water used to boil meat

INSTRUCTIONS:
a) Combine all ingredients, mix until smooth and pasty, and stuff into hog, beef or cloth casing.
b) Simmer in salted water for approximately 20 minutes.
c) Refrigerate for 24 hours before using.
d) Use it as a spread.

62. German Metz

INGREDIENTS:
- 4 pounds fine ground beef chuck
- 1 pounds fine ground bacon
- 1 tablespoon black pepper
- 1 teaspoon ground coriander
- 1 tablespoon salt
- 1 cup Rhine wine

INSTRUCTIONS:
a) Combine all ingredients, mix well, and stuff into hog casing.
b) Tie off in 6-inch lengths.
c) Cold smoke for 24 hours. To cook, fry or bake.

63. German Schwabischewurst

INGREDIENTS:
- 5 pounds fine ground pork butt
- 2 tablespoons salt
- 3 teaspoons black pepper
- 3 teaspoons sugar
- 6 cloves pressed garlic
- 2 tablespoons caraway seeds
- 1 cup cold water

INSTRUCTIONS:
a) Combine all ingredients, mix thoroughly, and stuff into hog casing.

b) To cook, bring to a boil and simmer approximately 40 minutes.

c) Bake, fry, or eat as is.

64. German Wurstchen

INGREDIENTS:
- 3 pounds medium ground pork butt
- 2 pounds medium ground veal
- 2 tablespoons salt
- 2 tablespoons black pepper
- 2 tablespoons pimento
- 2 teaspoons cardamon
- 1 cup Rhine wine

INSTRUCTIONS:
a) Combine all ingredients, mix well, and stuff into sheep casing.
b) Poach about 5 minutes, then broil.

65. Greek Loukanika Sausage

INGREDIENTS:
- 5 pounds coarse ground pork butt
- 3 teaspoons salt
- 7 cloves pressed garlic
- 1 tablespoon thyme
- 1 tablespoon marjoram
- 1½ teaspoons ground allspice
- 1½ teaspoons coriander
- 1 teaspoon crushed bay leaf
- 1½ tablespoons grated orange peel
- 1 cup red wine

INSTRUCTIONS:
a) Combine all ingredients, mix well, and stuff into hog casing, or make patties.

66. Greek Orange Sausage

INGREDIENTS:
- 3 pounds fine ground pork butt
- 2 pounds fine ground beef
- 3 cloves pressed garlic
- 1 large orange
- 1 tablespoon cinnamon
- 1 tablespoon allspice
- 1 tablespoon black pepper
- 1 tablespoon salt
- 1 cup white wine

INSTRUCTIONS:
a) Combine garlic, orange peel, cinnamon, allspice, pepper, salt, and wine.
b) Mix in blender until the orange peel is finely chopped.
c) Mix well into meat and stuff into hog casing, or make patties.

67. <u>Greek Pork Sausage</u>

INGREDIENTS:
- 5 pounds medium ground pork butt
- 1 large finely chopped onion
- 6 cloves pressed garlic
- 2 teaspoons black pepper
- 2 teaspoons oregano leaves
- $\frac{3}{4}$ teaspoons cayenne
- $\frac{3}{4}$ teaspoons chili powder
- $\frac{3}{4}$ teaspoons allspice
- $\frac{3}{4}$ teaspoons thyme
- 2 bay leaves
- $\frac{1}{2}$ cup chopped parsley
- 1 cup water

INSTRUCTIONS:
a) Combine all ingredients, mix well, and stuff into hog casing.
b) To cook, bake or fry.

68. Greek Blood Sausage

INGREDIENTS:
- 5 pounds coarse ground cooked pork butt (boiled)
- 2 tablespoons salt
- 1 cup grated onion
- 1 tablespoon black pepper
- $\frac{1}{2}$ teaspoons ground marjoram
- $\frac{1}{2}$ teaspoons ground thyme
- $\frac{1}{2}$ teaspoons mace
- $\frac{1}{2}$ teaspoons ground cloves
- 1 qt. pork blood

INSTRUCTIONS:
a) Combine all ingredients, mix well, and stuff into hog casing.

b) To cook, place sausage into tepid water and simmer for 15 minutes.

c) Add one teaspoons vinegar per quart of fresh blood to keep it from coagulating.

69. Hungarian Fish Sausage

INGREDIENTS:
- 4 white bread rolls
- 2 cups milk
- 5 pounds fish fillet
- 8 eggs
- 4 tablespoons parsley
- 2 teaspoons salt
- 1 teaspoon pepper

INSTRUCTIONS:
a) Soak rolls in milk, squeeze, shred, and mix the rolls with the fish, eggs, parsley, salt, and pepper, and stuff in sheep casing.
b) Fry or broil sausage.

70. Hungarian Hazi Kolbasz

INGREDIENTS:
- 5 pounds medium ground pork
- 4 cloves garlic
- 2 tablespoons salt
- 2 teaspoons black pepper
- 1½ tablespoons paprika
- ½ teaspoons ground cloves
- 1 lemon rind
- 1 cup water

INSTRUCTIONS:
a) Combine all ingredients and stuff into hog casing.
b) Bake about 1 hour at 350°F.

71. Hungarian Hurka

INGREDIENTS:
- 4 pounds pork butt
- 2 pounds pork heart
- 1 pounds pork jowl
- 1 pounds pork liver
- $\frac{1}{4}$ cup salt
- 1 tablespoon black pepper
- $\frac{1}{8}$ teaspoons ground marjoram
- 1 large onion fried in $\frac{1}{4}$ cup lard
- 5 pounds cooked rice

INSTRUCTIONS:
a) Cook and grind meat through coarse blade. Add 1 cup of juice from the boiled meat.

b) Mix all together and stuff into hog casing. Drop into boiling water. Boil for 1 minute, remove, and bake later.

72. Hungarian Kolbasz

INGREDIENTS:
- 12 pounds coarse ground pork
- 6 large cloves garlic
- $\frac{1}{4}$ cup salt
- 2 tablespoons black pepper
- 3 tablespoons paprika
- 1 teaspoon cayenne pepper
- 1 cup water

INSTRUCTIONS:
a) Cook garlic in water, then mash it.
b) Add liquid and garlic to other ingredients, and mix.
c) Stuff into hog casing.

73. Hungarian Majas Hurka (Hot Liver Sausage)

INGREDIENTS:
- 1 pounds pork butt
- 2 pounds pork liver
- 2 pounds pork lungs
- 2 tablespoons salt
- 1 cup uncooked rice
- $2\frac{1}{2}$ cups beef broth (bouillon)
- 2 large onions
- $\frac{1}{2}$ pounds lard
- 1 tablespoon pepper
- 1 teaspoon marjoram

INSTRUCTIONS:
a) Boil pork butt, liver, and lungs together with 1 tablespoon salt.
b) Cook rice in beef broth and fry onions until soft.
c) Combine all ingredients except the rice and put through the fine plate of the grinder.
d) Add rice, mix well, and stuff into hog casing. To cook, boil sausage for 10 minutes, then fry or bake.

74. Irish Sausage

INGREDIENTS:
- 5 pounds coarse ground pork butt
- 5 cups bread crumbs
- 4 eggs, lightly beaten
- 8 cloves pressed garlic
- 1 tablespoon salt
- 3 teaspoons thyme
- 3 teaspoons basil
- 3 teaspoons rosemary
- 3 teaspoons marjoram
- 3 teaspoons black pepper
- 2 cups water

INSTRUCTIONS:
a) Combine all ingredients, mix well, and stuff into sheep casing.
b) To cook, fry in butter or oil.

75. Irish Bologna

INGREDIENTS:
- 3 pounds beef chuck
- 2 pounds pork butt
- 2 tablespoons salt
- 1 tablespoon white pepper
- 4 cloves pressed garlic
- $\frac{1}{2}$ teaspoons ground coriander
- $\frac{1}{2}$ teaspoons ground ginger
- $\frac{1}{2}$ teaspoons ground mustard
- $\frac{1}{2}$ teaspoons ground nutmeg
- 2 cups water

INSTRUCTIONS:
a) Grind beef with half of the salt in coarse grinding plate, and allow to cure in refrigerator for about 48 hours.
b) Use the other half of the salt when putting pork through coarse grinding plate, and cure this overnight.
c) Regrind cured beef using fine plate, then add pork and grind mixture again. Add spices and water and stir heartily until the whole mixture has become sticky. It may take you 30-40 minutes to reach this consistency.
d) Stuff the sausage into beef casing or muslin bags and hang in a cool place overnight.
e) Smoke at about 115°F for 2 hours or until a rich mahogany brown.
f) Put the hot, freshly smoked sausage immediately into water heated to about 170°F, and cook it until it

squeaks when the pressure of the thumb and finger on the casing is suddenly released.

g) The usual cooking time for sausage stuffed in beef intestine is 15-30 minutes—for larger casing, 60-90 minutes.

h) Plunge the cooked sausage into cold water and chill it. Hang in a cool place.

76. Italian Cooked Salami

INGREDIENTS:
- 2½ pounds fine ground beef chuck
- 2½ pounds fine ground pork butt
- 3 tablespoons salt
- 5 tablespoons honey
- 1 tablespoon black pepper
- 3 teaspoons whole black pepper
- 1 tablespoon cardamom
- 10 cloves pressed garlic
- 1 cup dry nonfat milk
- 1 cup water

INSTRUCTIONS:
a) Combine all ingredients, mix well, and refrigerate for 24 hours.
b) Stuff into cellulose or fiber casing. Cool smoke for 1-2 hours or until the casing is dry.
c) Gradually increase the temperature of the smokehouse to 160°-165°F.
d) Lightly smoke until an internal temperature of 140°F is reached.
e) Chill the sausage in cold water and hang at room temperature 2-3 hours.
f) Refrigerate.

77. <u>Italian Cotechino</u>

INGREDIENTS:
- 5 pounds coarse ground fresh ham with skin
- 2 tablespoons salt
- 1⅓ tablespoons coarse black pepper
- 2 teaspoons ground nutmeg
- 2 teaspoons ground cinnamon
- 2 teaspoons cayenne pepper
- ½ cup parmesan cheese
- 1 teaspoon ground cloves
- 1 cup cold water

INSTRUCTIONS:
a) Combine all ingredients, mix well, and stuff into hog casing.
b) Allow 2 days in the refrigerator before eating or freezing.

78. Italian Luganega

INGREDIENTS:
- 5 pounds fine ground pork butt
- 1½ cups grated parmesan cheese
- ⅔ teaspoons ground nutmeg
- ⅔ teaspoons ground coriander
- ½ teaspoons grated lemon peel
- ½ teaspoons grated orange peel
- 1¼ teaspoons black pepper
- 2 cloves pressed garlic
- 1 tablespoon salt
- 1 cup dry vermouth

INSTRUCTIONS:
a) Combine all ingredients, mix well, and stuff into hog casing.

b) Let stand in the refrigerator 1 or 2 days before freezing.

79. Italian Pepper Sausage

INGREDIENTS:
- 4½ pounds coarse ground pork
- 1½ pounds salt pork
- 1 clove garlic
- 1 onion, quartered
- 1½ tablespoons freshly ground black pepper
- 2 tablespoons salt
- 4 tablespoons paprika
- 4 teaspoons fennel
- 2 tablespoons crushed red pepper, dried
- ¼ teaspoons thyme
- ½ teaspoons bay leaf, crushed
- ¼ teaspoons coriander
- 1 cup red wine

INSTRUCTIONS:
a) Combine all ingredients, mix well, and stuff into hog casing.
b) You may split lengthwise and broil under medium heat, or pan-fry until brown on all sides and well done.

80. <u>Italian Sausage</u>

INGREDIENTS:
- 5 pounds coarse ground pork butt
- 1 tablespoon salt
- 1 tablespoon coarse black pepper
- 5 cloves pressed garlic
- 1 tablespoon fennel seeds
- 1 teaspoon anise seed
- 1 cup cold water

INSTRUCTIONS:
a) Add 1 tablespoon crushed hot pepper for hotter-style sausage.

b) Combine all ingredients, mix well, and stuff into hog casing or make patties.

81. Italian Sausage (Hot)

INGREDIENTS:
- 5 pounds coarse ground pork butt
- 2 tablespoons salt
- 2 teaspoons fennel seed
- 2 teaspoons sugar
- 1 tablespoon crushed hot pepper
- $\frac{1}{2}$ teaspoons caraway seed
- 2 teaspoons coriander
- 1 cup water

INSTRUCTIONS:
a) Combine all ingredients, mix well, and stuff into hog casing.
b) To cook, fry or bake.

82. Italian Sausage (Sweet)

INGREDIENTS:
- 5 pounds coarse ground pork butt
- 3 teaspoons fennel seed
- 2 teaspoons white pepper
- 1½ teaspoons sage leaves
- 5 cloves pressed garlic
- 3 teaspoons salt
- 1 cup white wine

INSTRUCTIONS:

a) Combine all ingredients, mix well, and stuff into hog casing or make patties.

83. Italian Sausage (Sweet Or Hot)

INGREDIENTS:
- 5 pounds coarse ground pork butt
- 1⅓ tablespoons salt
- 1½ tablespoons coarsely ground black pepper
- 1⅓ tablespoons ground coriander
- 5 cloves pressed garlic
- 2 tablespoons paprika
- 1 cup cold water

INSTRUCTIONS:
a) Add 2 teaspoons crushed red peppers for hot sausage.
b) Combine all ingredients, mix well, and stuff into hog casing or make patties.

84. Italian chorizo

INGREDIENTS:
- 5 pounds coarse ground pork butt
- ½ cup red wine vinegar
- 1 large chopped onion
- 5 cloves pressed garlic
- 1 tablespoon salt
- 3 teaspoons brown sugar
- 1½ teaspoons cumin
- ½ teaspoons coriander
- 1 teaspoon dried mint leaves
- 1 tablespoon oregano
- 1 teaspoon basil
- 3 tablespoons chili powder
- 1 cup water

INSTRUCTIONS:
a) Combine all ingredients, mix well, and stuff into hog casing.

85. Mexican Sonora Chorizo

INGREDIENTS:
- 5 pounds coarse ground pork butt
- 6 cloves pressed garlic
- 1 small diced onion
- 2 tablespoons pimentos
- 2 tablespoons chili powder (or more)
- $\frac{1}{4}$ cup brandy
- $\frac{1}{4}$ cup vinegar
- 1 teaspoon black pepper
- $\frac{1}{2}$ teaspoons cinnamon
- $1\frac{1}{2}$ teaspoons cumin
- $1\frac{1}{2}$ tablespoons salt
- 1 cup water

INSTRUCTIONS:
a) Combine all ingredients, mix well, and stuff into hog casing.

86. Mexican Chorizo

INGREDIENTS:
- 5 pounds coarse ground pork butt
- 5 teaspoons salt
- 2 teaspoons black pepper
- 1 tablespoon chili powder
- 2 teaspoons crushed hot peppers, dried
- 2 teaspoons ground cumin
- 2 tablespoons paprika
- 2 large minced onions
- 8 cloves pressed garlic
- 1 cup cold water

INSTRUCTIONS:
a) Combine all ingredients, mix well, and stuff into hog casing or make patties. And stuff into hog casing, or make patties.
b) Wait.

87. Mexican/Spanish Lamb Sausage

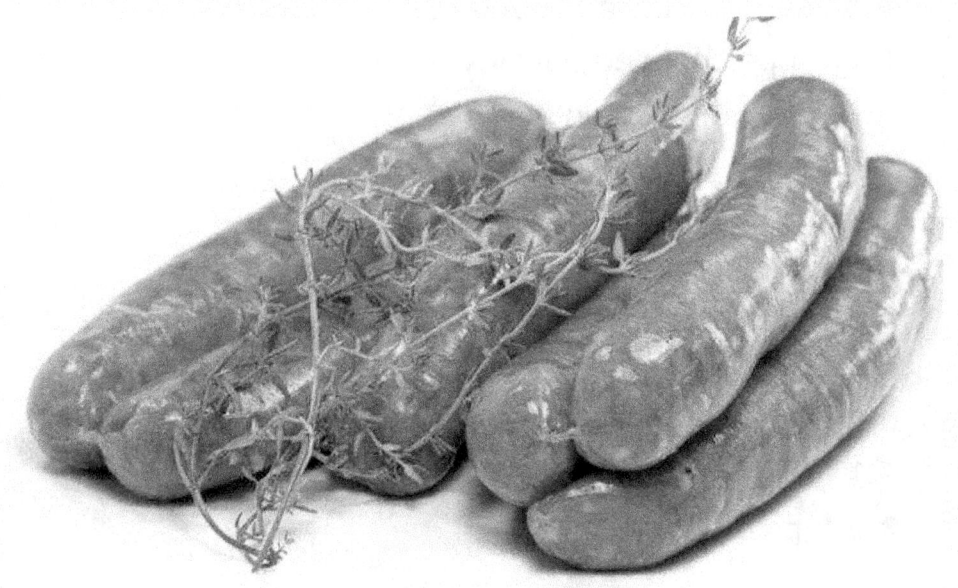

INGREDIENTS:
- 5 pounds coarse ground lamb
- $1\frac{3}{4}$ cups chopped parsley
- $1\frac{3}{4}$ cups minced onion
- 2 teaspoons marjoram
- $\frac{1}{2}$ teaspoons cumin
- $1\frac{1}{2}$ teaspoons coriander
- 2 teaspoons oregano
- 3 teaspoons cayenne
- 3 teaspoons black pepper
- 1 tablespoon salt
- 1 cup cold water

INSTRUCTIONS:
a) Combine all ingredients, mix well, and stuff into sheep casing.
b) To cook, broil, barbecue (very nice), or bake.

88. Norwegian Sausage

INGREDIENTS:
- 3 pounds coarse ground beef chuck
- 2 pounds coarse ground pork butt
- 1½ tablespoons salt
- 4 medium onions, grated
- 1 tablespoon black pepper
- 2½ teaspoons nutmeg
- 1 cup cold water

INSTRUCTIONS:
a) Combine all ingredients, mix well, and stuff into hog casing.
b) To cook, bake or fry.

89. Polish Blood Sausage

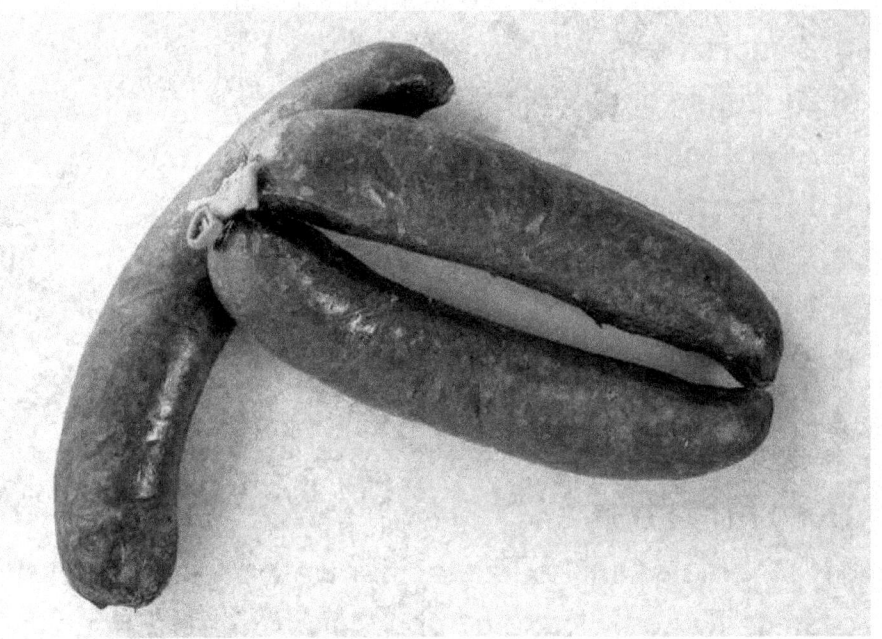

INGREDIENTS:
- 2½ pounds coarse ground pork butt
- 2 quarts pig's blood
- 2½ cups cooked rice or barley
- 1 teaspoon ginger
- 1½ teaspoons black pepper
- 1½ teaspoons allspice
- 1 tablespoon salt
- 3 cloves pressed garlic
- 2 teaspoons baking powder

INSTRUCTIONS:
a) Combine all ingredients, mix well, and stuff into hog casing. To cook, bake at about 375°F for 1 hour.
b) Add one teaspoons vinegar per quart of fresh blood to keep it from coagulating.

90. Polish Kielbasa

INGREDIENTS:
- 5 pounds coarse ground pork
- 2 tablespoons salt
- 1½ teaspoons pepper
- 1 teaspoon marjoram
- 3 cloves garlic, finely chopped
- 1 cup water

INSTRUCTIONS:
a) Combine all ingredients, mix well, and stuff into hog casing.
b) To cook, cover partially and simmer for 1½ hours.

91. Polish Kiszka

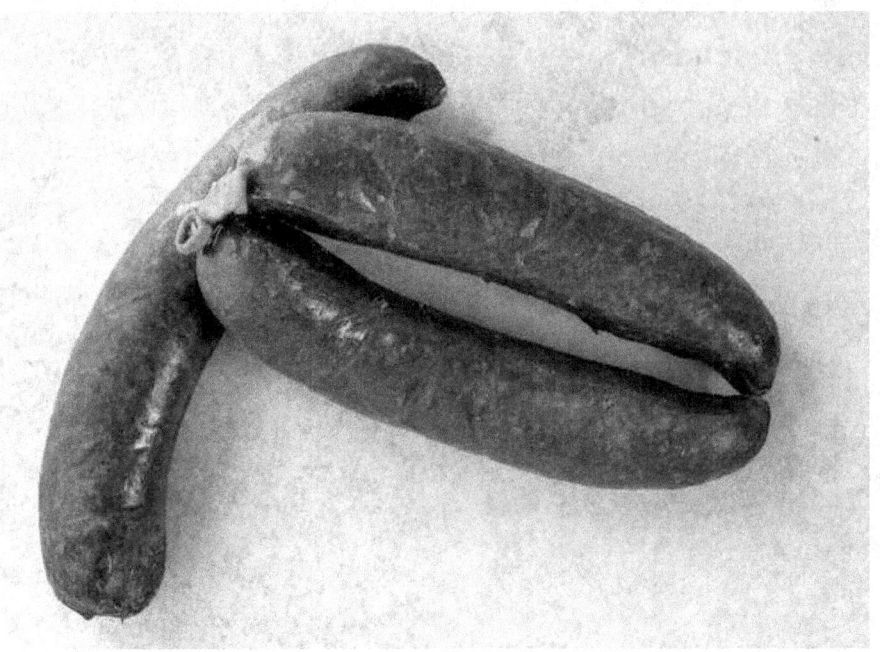

INGREDIENTS:
- 3 pounds coarse ground cooked pork butt
- 2 pounds cooked buckwheat
- $\frac{1}{2}$ teaspoons marjoram
- 1 tablespoon salt
- 1 tablespoon black pepper

INSTRUCTIONS:
a) Combine all ingredients, mix well, and stuff into hog casing.
b) To cook, bake or as you please.

92. Polish Kiszka z Krwia

INGREDIENTS:
- 4 split pig's feet
- 3 pounds cubed pork butt
- 7 onions
- 3 pounds cubed pork liver
- 5 pounds buckwheat
- 1 tablespoon ground allspice
- 2 tablespoons ground marjoram
- $2\frac{1}{2}$ tablespoons salt
- 2 tablespoons black pepper
- 1 pt. pig's blood (add last)

INSTRUCTIONS:
a) Cook together all ingredients.
b) Combine all ingredients and cook until done (except the blood).
c) Cool and add the blood. Mix well and stuff into hog casing. Bake until done. Wonderful!
d) Add one teaspoons vinegar per quart of fresh blood to keep it from coagulating.

93. Polish Sausage

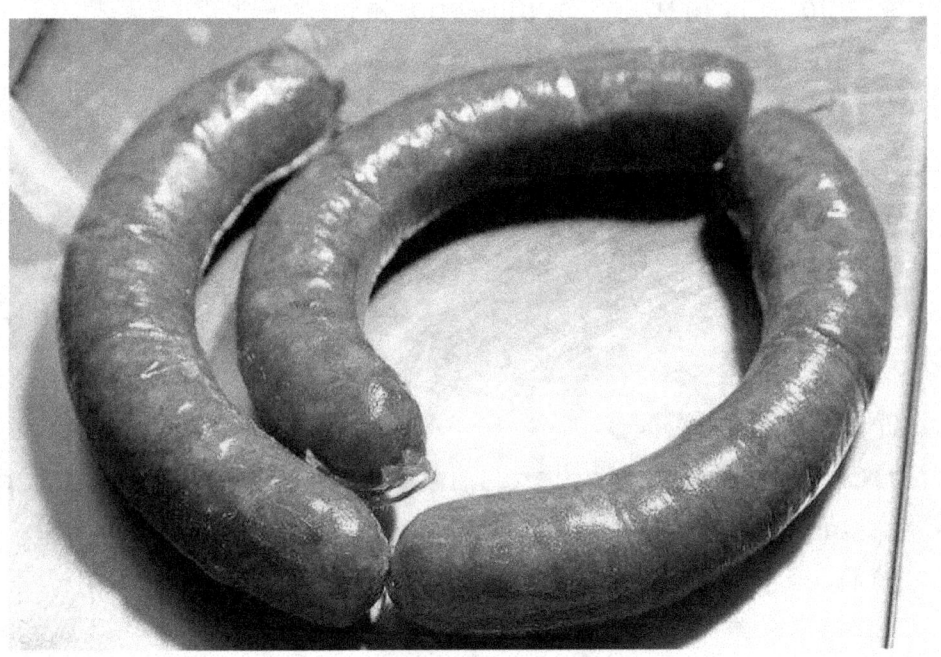

INGREDIENTS:
- 5 pounds medium ground pork butt
- 1½ tablespoons salt
- 1 tablespoon sugar
- 1 tablespoon black pepper
- 1 teaspoon marjoram
- 4 cloves pressed garlic
- 1 cup water

INSTRUCTIONS:
a) Combine all ingredients, mix well, and stuff into hog casing.
b) To cook, bake or fry.

94. Smoked Polish Kielbasa

INGREDIENTS:
- 5 pounds fine ground pork butt
- 3 tablespoons salt
- 1 tablespoon sugar
- 1 tablespoon black pepper
- 8 cloves pressed garlic
- 1 teaspoon marjoram
- 1 cup water

INSTRUCTIONS:
a) Combine all ingredients, mix well, and refrigerate for 24 hours.
b) Stuff into large hog casing.
c) Cool smoke for 1-2 hours or until the casing is dry. Gradually increase the temperature of the smokehouse to 160°-165°F.
d) Apply a heavy smoke until an internal temperature of 140°F is reached.
e) Chill the sausage in cold water and hang at room temperature 2-3 hours.

95. Portuguese Linguiça

INGREDIENTS:
- 5 pounds coarse ground pork butt
- 2 tablespoons salt
- 1 tablespoon sugar
- 8 cloves pressed garlic
- $\frac{1}{4}$ cup wine vinegar
- 4 tablespoons paprika
- 1 tablespoon black pepper
- 3 teaspoons marjoram
- 1 cup red wine

INSTRUCTIONS:
a) Combine all ingredients and mix well.
b) Stuff into hog casing.
c) To cook, fry in Rhine wine or bake.

96. Romanian Beef Sausage

INGREDIENTS:
- 5 pounds coarse ground beef chuck
- 5 teaspoons salt
- 1 teaspoon pepper
- 5 cloves pressed garlic
- 1 tablespoon soda
- $1\frac{1}{2}$ teaspoons cloves
- 1 cup water
- 2 tablespoons sugar

INSTRUCTIONS:
a) Combine all ingredients, mix well, and stuff into hog casing.

97. Romanian Mititei

INGREDIENTS:
- 5 pounds medium ground beef chuck
- 8 cloves pressed garlic
- 3 teaspoons baking soda
- 1 tablespoon salt
- 1 tablespoon black pepper
- 1 cup chopped parsley
- ⅔ cup olive oil
- 1 cup warm water

INSTRUCTIONS:
a) Combine all ingredients, mix well, and stuff into hog casing.
b) To cook, barbecue, broil, or bake.

98. Romanian Pork And Beef Sausage

INGREDIENTS:
- 3 pounds medium ground pork butt
- 2 pounds medium ground beef chuck
- 6 cloves pressed garlic
- 1½ tablespoons salt
- 2 teaspoons black pepper
- ½ teaspoons marjoram
- ½ teaspoons lovage
- 1 cup water

INSTRUCTIONS:
a) Combine all ingredients, mix well, and stuff into hog casing.
b) Broil or bake.

99. Russian Sausage

INGREDIENTS:
- 5 pounds coarse ground pork butt
- 2 large chopped onions
- 2 tablespoons pressed garlic
- 1 cup fresh parsley, chopped
- 3 tablespoons dill seeds
- 3 tablespoons caraway seeds
- 1 tablespoon black pepper
- 1 tablespoon salt
- 2 cups water

INSTRUCTIONS:

a) Combine all ingredients, mix well, and stuff into hog casing.
b) Bake at 350°F, approximately 1 hour.

100. Scottish Haggis

INGREDIENTS:
- 1 sheep's stomach
- 1 sheep's heart
- 1 sheep's lungs
- 1 sheep's liver
- $\frac{3}{4}$ cup oatmeal
- $\frac{1}{2}$ pounds fresh beef suet
- 3 onions, chopped
- 1 teaspoon salt
- $\frac{1}{8}$ teaspoons pepper
- pinch of cayenne
- $\frac{3}{4}$ cup stock
- 1 cup whiskey

INSTRUCTIONS:
a) Wash stomach thoroughly, turn inside out, and scald in boiling water. Scrape with knife. Soak overnight in cold salt water.
b) Simmer heart, lungs, and liver for $1\frac{1}{2}$ hours. Cool.
c) Toast oatmeal in oven.
d) Cut away gristle and pipes, and grate liver coarsely.
e) Chop heart and lungs and mix all ingredients together.
f) Add more salt and pepper if desired. Fill stomach two-thirds full.
g) There should be room for the oatmeal to swell.
h) Press air from bag and sew securely.
i) Prick stomach several times with a needle.
j) Boil for 3 hours uncovered.
k) Add water as needed. Remove threads and serve with a spoon.

CONCLUSION

Congratulations, you've reached the end of The Ultimate Sausage Making Cookbook! We hope that you've enjoyed exploring the world of homemade sausages and that you've discovered some new favorite recipes along the way.

We know that making sausages can be a daunting task for some, but we hope that this cookbook has demystified the process and given you the confidence to try new things in the kitchen. Whether you're a seasoned pro or a newbie, making your own sausages is a rewarding and satisfying experience that is sure to impress your friends and family.

Remember, the key to successful sausage making is to use high-quality ingredients and to follow the recipes closely. Don't be afraid to experiment with different flavors and seasonings to create your own unique recipes.

And if you enjoyed this cookbook, be sure to check out our other titles for more delicious recipes and culinary inspiration.

Thanks for joining us on this journey, and happy sausage making!

www.ingramcontent.com/pod-product-compliance
Lightning Source LLC
Chambersburg PA
CBHW050354120526
44590CB00015B/1688